BOSTON BRUINS

The Original 6

Eric Zweig

Crabtree Publishing Company

www.crabtreebooks.com

Celebrating Hockey's History

The Original 6

Author: Eric Zweig,
  Member of the Society for International
  Hockey Research

Editor: Ellen Rodger

Editorial director: Kathy Middleton

Design: Tammy McGarr

Photo research: Tammy McGarr

Proofreader: Wendy Scavuzzo

**Production coordinator and
  Prepress technician:** Tammy McGarr

Print coordinator: Margaret Amy Salter

Library and Archives Canada Cataloguing in Publication

Zweig, Eric, 1963-, author
  Boston Bruins / Eric Zweig.

(The original six : celebrating hockey's history)
Includes index.
Issued in print and electronic formats.
ISBN 978-0-7787-3426-0 (hardcover).--
ISBN 978-0-7787-3442-0 (softcover).--
ISBN 978-1-4271-1921-6 (HTML)

  1. Boston Bruins (Hockey team)--Juvenile literature.
2. Boston Bruins (Hockey team)--History--Juvenile literature.
I. Title.

GV848.B68Z84 2017   j796.962'640974461   C2017-903475-8
                                                C2017-903476-6

Library of Congress Cataloging-in-Publication Data

Names: Zweig, Eric, 1963- author.
Title: Boston Bruins / Eric Zweig.
Description: New York : Crabtree Publishing Company, [2018] |
  Series: The Original Six: Celebrating hockey's history |
  Includes index. | Audience: Ages: 10-14. | Audience: Grades: 7 to 8.
Identifiers: LCCN 2017029650 (print) | LCCN 2017033899 (ebook) |
  ISBN 9781427119216 (Electronic HTML) |
  ISBN 9780778734260 (Reinforced library binding) |
  ISBN 9780778734420 (Paperback)
Subjects: LCSH: Boston Bruins (Hockey team)--History--Juvenile
  literature. | National Hockey League--History--Juvenile literature. |
  Hockey--History--Juvenile literature.
Classification: LCC GV848.B6 (ebook) | LCC GV848.B6 Z94 2018 (print)
  | DDC 796.962/640974461--dc23
LC record available at https://lccn.loc.gov/2017029650

Crabtree Publishing Company
www.crabtreebooks.com   1-800-387-7650

Printed in the USA/102017/CG20170907

Published in Canada
Crabtree Publishing
616 Welland Ave.
St. Catharines, Ontario
L2M 5V6

Published in the United States
Crabtree Publishing
PMB 59051
350 Fifth Avenue, 59th Floor
New York, New York 10118

Published in the United Kingdom
Crabtree Publishing
Maritime House
Basin Road North, Hove
BN41 1WR

Published in Australia
Crabtree Publishing
3 Charles Street
Coburg North
VIC, 3058

Table of Contents

Celebrating Hockey's History

The Original 6

THE NHL AT 100

Charles Francis Adams had a dream. His dream was a team: a professional hockey club in Boston, Massachusetts, that would compete with the best of them in the National Hockey League (NHL). He made that dream happen in record time, buying a **franchise,** hiring an ace coach and manager, and building a team. All this happened within just a few months in 1924.

Boston joins the NHL

Charles Adams owned a chain of grocery stores and he loved hockey. In 1924 Adams attended the Stanley Cup Finals in Montreal that pitted the Canadiens against the Calgary Tigers. Adams decided that his home town of Boston needed an NHL team. So he paid $15,000 and bought the **rights**. His team, the Boston Bruins, hit the ice for their first official league game on Dec. 1, 1924.

The Boston Bruins played their very first game on November 27, 1924. It was an exhibition game against the Saskatoon Sheiks of the Western Canada Hockey League. The Bruins lost 2–1.

Boston Bruins
1929-30

Victoria rink in 1893

And Then There Was a Trophy!

Hockey History

The NHL was formed just seven years earlier in November 1917. For its first six seasons, all the teams were based in Canadian cities. When the league began to think about expanding into the United States, the long history of hockey in Boston made it an obvious choice. Of course, the history of hockey itself began long before the NHL. People have played hockey-like games with balls and sticks since ancient times. Some writers claim that the first organized ice hockey games were played on ponds in Nova Scotia in 1800. That's just a hop, skip, and long jump away from Boston, where schools soon organized teams in the late 1800s. Others say the first indoor hockey game on record was held at the Victoria Skating Rink in Montreal in 1875. Victoria Rink was also the location of the first Stanley Cup Playoffs in 1894.

More than 20,000 people attend Stanley Cup Finals today. Another three million may watch it on television. Back in 1893, the cup was first presented at a meeting of the Montreal Amateur Athletic Association. It's not likely that many people attended. Hockey's **Holy Grail** was the **brainchild** of Canada's Governor-General, Lord Stanley of Preston. He bought and donated a trophy to the winner of the amateur competition, Dominion Hockey Challenge Cup. Over time, the cup became the top award for professional hockey.

IN THE BEGINNING

Who would have thought the NHL owes its beginnings to a fight? Not a knock 'em sock 'em hockey brawl, but a simmering grudge match between hockey team owners. The feud began in 1915 between Eddie Livingstone and his fellow National Hockey Association team owners. Two years later, the other owners formed a new league without him. That league was the NHL.

League of Its Own

The National Hockey Association was a professional hockey league that existed before the NHL. Livingstone was owner of an NHA **franchise**, the Toronto Blueshirts. He liked to argue and repeatedly clashed with other team owners over games and players. To end the disagreements, the other owners met in Montreal and formed the NHL. They did not ask Livingstone to join. The NHL started with four teams, the Ottawa Senators, Quebec Bulldogs, Montreal Wanderers, and Montreal Canadiens. The Toronto Arenas joined after Quebec dropped out, and eventually were renamed the St. Patricks. But just three teams finished out the NHL's first season. That's a long way from the 31 teams that are in the league 100 years later.

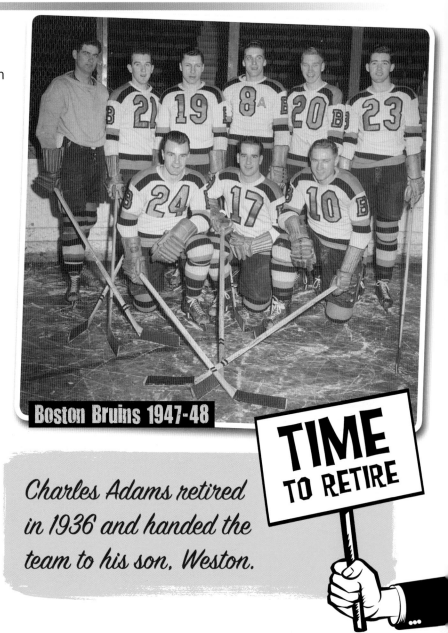

Boston Bruins 1947-48

Charles Adams retired in 1936 and handed the team to his son, Weston.

TIME TO RETIRE

Slow Growth

The NHL struggled through its first season of 1917–18, but things got better. By its third season of 1919–20, the league was back up to four teams when the Quebec Bulldogs joined the Montreal Canadiens, the Toronto St. Pats, and the Ottawa Senators. Quebec dropped out after just one season, but the team was replaced by the Hamilton Tigers. Two more teams were added for the 1924–25 season: the Montreal Maroons and the Boston Bruins. The Bruins proved that American fans would come out to watch Canadian teams play hockey, so the NHL began to add more teams in the United States. For the 1925–26 season, a team called the Pittsburgh Pirates joined the NHL. The Hamilton Tigers were replaced that year by a team in New York called the Americans. In 1926–27, the NHL added another New York team known as the Rangers. Chicago and Detroit also joined the NHL that season. A league that once had only three teams, with all of them in Canada, had grown to 10 teams with six of them in the United States.

Eddie Shore, George Owen, and Lionel Hitchman of the Bruins, 1928-29

Original 6

Toronto Maple Leafs
Boston Bruins
New York Rangers
Detroit Red Wings
Montreal Canadiens
Chicago Black Hawks
(now Blackhawks)

When the stock market crashed in 1929, the world was plunged into an economic disaster known as the **Great Depression**. With businesses closed and so many people out of work, people didn't have the money to buy tickets to hockey games. By the start of the 1942–43 season, the NHL was down to just the Bruins, Rangers, Red Wings, Black Hawks, Canadiens, and Maple Leafs. These were the only teams in the NHL for 25 seasons until the league began to expand again in 1967. They are often referred to as "The Original Six."

THE STANLEY CUP

Original Cup

The original bowl was bought from a silversmith's shop in London, England, for 10 guineas ($50).

10 guineas

The cup's donor was Lord Stanley of Preston, Canada's 6th governor general (1888-1893). Stanley's sons and daughter played amateur hockey in Canada.

The cup has a $70,000 insurance value today

Each player on the winning team gets their own special day with the Stanley Cup during the summer.

1927
The first year the Boston Bruins played for the Stanley Cup. They lost to the Ottawa Senators.

1941
The Bruins became the first team to sweep four straight games in the Stanley Cup Finals in 1941.

The Isobel Cup and the Isobel Gathorne-Hardy Award are awards given to female hockey players in the National Women's Hockey League. The awards are named after the hockey-loving daughter (in white) of Lord Stanley. Boston Pride won the first Isobel Cup championship in 2016. The Isobel Gathorne-Hardy Award is awarded to any female player in Canada who shows leadership qualities.

There are 3 cups:

- The original Challenge Cup from 1893,
- The Presentation Cup given to championship teams since 1963,
- The replica Presentation Cup created in 1993 and used as a "stand-in" for the cup at the Hockey Hall of Fame.

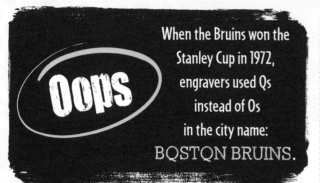

When the Bruins won the Stanley Cup in 1972, engravers used Qs instead of Os in the city name: BQSTQN BRUINS.

1st The Bruins became the first team in NHL history to win three seven-game series in one playoff year when they won the Stanley Cup in 2011.

The Stanley Cup is usually presented to the team captain on the ice after the last game of the finals. Boston didn't have a captain in 1970 or 1972, so the trophy was presented to their longest-serving player, John Bucyk.

Boston's Stanley Cup Winning Years

1929 over New York Rangers
1939 over Toronto Maple Leafs
1941 over Detroit Red Wings
1970 over St. Louis Blues
1972 over New York Rangers
2011 over Vancouver Canucks

6

39 The Bruins' 2011 Stanley Cup win came after a 39-year cup drought.

The Bruins' win over the Rangers in 1929 marked the first time in hockey history that two American-based teams played for the Stanley Cup.

1,000,000+

More than one million fans attended the 2011 Stanley Cup championship parade in Boston—the largest championship parade in the city's history.

IN TIMMY THOMAS Ⓑ WE TRUST

BIG, BAD BRUINS

When Boston officially joined the NHL on November 1, 1924, owner Charles Adams wanted a tough team. He wanted its name to reflect a big, strong, smart, and ferocious animal. "Bruin" was a Dutch word for "brown" that was used in old English folk tales to mean a brown bear. So Boston's team became the Bruins.

First Coach and GM

Hockey fans today know Art Ross as the name of the NHL trophy given to the league's scoring leader. More than 100 years ago, Ross was known as one of the best players in hockey. He was a star defenseman who played most of his career before the NHL was formed. In 1924, he was hired by the Bruins to be their coach and general manager.

1940-41 Stanley Cup Team

Quick Ascent

Like a lot of **expansion** teams, the Bruins struggled at first. They finished dead last in the NHL during their first season of 1924–25. Ross quickly built the tough and talented team that Charles Adams wanted. Led by players such as Eddie Shore on defense, Cooney Weiland, Dit Clapper, Bill Cowley, and Milt Schmidt as forwards, and Tiny Thompson and Frank Brimsek in goal, Boston became a powerhouse. The Bruins finished in first place in their own division, or in the overall NHL standings, 10 times in 14 seasons from 1927 to 1941, and won the Stanley Cup three times.

Back on Top

The Bruins had some good teams in the 1950s, but then struggled badly. They missed the playoffs eight seasons in a row from 1959 to 1967. After the NHL doubled in size with six new expansion teams in 1967–68, Boston was ready to explode. Led this time by Bobby Orr on defense and Phil Esposito at center, the Bruins boasted the NHL's best offense and won the Stanley Cup again in 1970 and 1972. Although it took until 2011 for Boston to claim the cup again, the Bruins have almost always ranked among the NHL's best teams since the 1970s.

Hoisting the cup after a Stanley Cup Finals win is an NHL tradition. Boston goalie Tim Thomas makes the cup look like it weighs nothing, while teammate Patrice Bergeron moves in for a hearty hug after Boston's game-7 win over the Vancouver Canucks in 2011.

Bruins and Maroons, Boston Garden, 1929-30

Best Ever?

In a 44-game season back in 1929–30, the Bruins had a record of 38 wins, 5 losses, and 1 tie1 for 77 points. It took until 1950–51, when the NHL season had grown to 70 games, for any team to win more than 38 games. Boston's winning percentage of .875 in 1929–30 has never been beaten. In today's modern 82-game season, a team would need to get 144 points to break Boston's record!

11

BOSTON BY THE NUMBERS

Bruins linemates **Milt Schmidt**, **Woody Dumart**, and **Bobby Bauer** took the top three spots in the NHL scoring race in **1939-40**.

Boston teammates **Phil Esposito**, **Bobby Orr**, **John Bucyk**, and **Ken Hodge** took the top four spots in the NHL scoring race in **1970-71**. **Esposito**, **Orr**, **Hodge**, and **Wayne Cashman** finished **1-2-3-4** in **1973-74**.

When Brad Marchand came in sixth in the NHL scoring race in 2016-17, it marked the highest finish by a Boston player in a full season since former Bruin Joe Thornton finished third in 2002-03.

Bruins Regular-Season Franchise Leaders (Career)

Games	Goals	Assists	Points	Wins	Shutouts	Goals-Against Average
1,518	545	1,111	1,506	252	74	1.99
Raymond Bourque	John Bucyk	Raymond Bourque	Raymond Bourque	Tiny Thompson	Tiny Thompson	Tiny Thompson

Teams retire sweater or jersey numbers to honor top players who have left the team, retired (sometimes through career-ending injuries), or died.

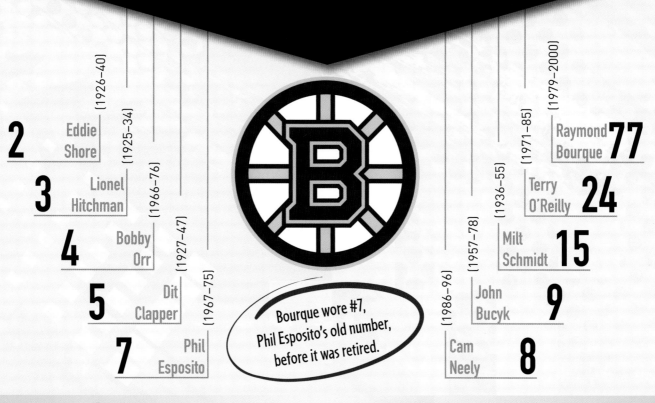

2 Eddie Shore (1926–40)

3 Lionel Hitchman (1925–34)

4 Bobby Orr (1966–76)

5 Dit Clapper (1927–47)

7 Phil Esposito (1967–75)

Bourque wore #7, Phil Esposito's old number, before it was retired.

Raymond Bourque **77** (1979–2000)

Terry O'Reilly **24** (1971–85)

Milt Schmidt **15** (1936–55)

John Bucyk **9** (1957–78)

Cam Neely **8** (1986–96)

20 Seasons

Seasons with the Boston Bruins for Dit Clapper (1927–47). He was the first player in NHL history to play that long.

100 Points

Points in one season first hit by Phil Esposito on March 2, 1969. Esposito finished the 1968–69 season with 49 goals and 77 assists for 126 points.

Bruins Franchise Leaders (Season)

Goals	Assists	Points	Wins	Shutouts	Goals-Against Average
76	**102**	**152**	**40**	**15**	**1.15**
Phil Esposito (1970–71)	Bobby Orr (1970–71)	Phil Esposito (1970–71)	Pete Peeters (1982–83)	Hal Winkler (1927–28)	Tiny Thompson (1928–29)

BLACK, WHITE, AND GOLD

Rumor has it that Charles Adams had a thing for brown. Originally, the Bruins' uniforms were brown and gold because those were the colors associated with the chain of grocery stores Adams owned. Later, both the Bruins and the stores changed the brown to black.

Lookin' Good

For their first season in 1924–25, the Boston Bruins wore brown sweaters with two yellow stripes on the arms and a third yellow stripe around the waist. They also had brown socks with two yellow stripes. For the next few years, Bruins sweaters were white and brown with yellow stripes. The logo on the chest was a side view of a brown bear with BOSTON arching above it and BRUINS in a straight line below. Beginning in 1932, the logo on the sweater was a large capital B.

Black replaced brown on the Bruins' sweaters and socks in 1934. From 1936 to 1948, the Bruins wore their numbers on the front and back of their sweaters (the way football teams do) with a B logo on each shoulder. From 1940 to 1944, they sometimes wore gold sweaters with the word BRUINS written in fancy script across the chest.

Spoked-B Logo

To celebrate the team's 25th season in 1948–49, the team introduced a new logo featuring a B inside of a circle with spokes. After a little tinkering with it the following season, the Bruins have been wearing pretty much the same spoked-B logo to this day! In fact, the entire Bruins uniform has looked pretty much the same since the mid-1950s—except that sometimes the main color has been white, sometimes it's been black, and sometimes it's been gold.

First Helmet Heads

Bruins players were the first in NHL history to wear helmets. George Owen joined the team in 1928–29 and is often credited as the first to wear a helmet. Owen, Eddie Shore, and Lionel Hitchman all wore helmets during a rough playoff series against the Montreal Maroons in 1930. In January 1934, Toronto's Ace Bailey suffered a fractured skull that ended his career during a game at Boston. After that, Bruins boss Art Ross designed new helmets to protect all his players. Everyone had to wear them. Even goalie Tiny Thompson wore a helmet, despite the fact that goalies didn't wear masks at the time! Boston's helmets didn't catch on, and it would not be until 1979 that the NHL passed new rules saying that players had to wear helmets.

The helmet worn by Eddie Shore during his first game back after his suspension from the hit to Toronto's Ace Bailey.

Shoulders, arms, and chest

Shoulder pads were strips of material in the 1920s. Today, players wear molded protectors for chest and shoulders, plus elbow pads and slash guards.

Gloves

In the early years of the NHL, gloves ran up to the forearm. Today's gloves cover just past the wrist. Wrist protectors are also worn.

Pants and guards

Lightweight padded pants protect the hips, thighs, and tailbone. Players began wearing leather elbow and forearm pads in the 1930s. Shin guards now protect the knee and lower leg.

Visors

Plastic visors protect eyes from sticks and elbows.

Mouthguards

Missing teeth are still common in the NHL. Mouthguards worn during games may also help protect against concussions.

Stick

The old sticks were wooden. Many current sticks are made from a combination of materials that make them light and strong.

Skates

Skates used to be leather boots with attached blades. Today's skates are **synthetic** boots that offer foot and ankle protection.

On Home Ice

The Boston Arena

- Bruins first home in the NHL from 1924–25 through 1927–28.

- Originally opened in 1910, the Boston Arena was destroyed by fire in 1918 and rebuilt in 1919 to open again in 1920.

December 1918

- Known today as Matthews Arena, the rink is still used for hockey by the men's and women's teams at Northeastern University.

- It could hold about 9,000 fans after it was expanded in 1926. Today it holds 4,666 for hockey.

Boston Garden

- First Bruins home game was November 20, 1928. The Montreal Canadiens beat Boston 1-0.

- The last Bruins game was a preseason game on September 26, 1995. The New Jersey Devils beat Boston 3-2.

- Cost of construction is said to have been as high as $10 million or as low as $4 million. That would be equivalent to about $56 million today.

- Boston Garden was built before the NHL set a standard size for rinks of 200 feet by 85 feet (61 m × 26 m). It was only 191 by 83 (58.2 m × 25.3 m).

- Original seating capacity was 13,909 for hockey. With standing room, it could hold close to 16,000.

- Maximum seating was 15,003 from 1972 to 1975. There were 14,448 seats when Boston Garden closed.

- In addition to hockey, Boston Garden was the home of basketball's Boston Celtics of the NBA from 1946 to 1995. In 1957, it became the first arena to host the Stanley Cup Final and NBA Finals at the same time. This happened again in 1958 and 1974.

- The Boston Garden was torn down in 1997.

 **TD Garden**

 It was originally called the FleetCenter when the Bruins played their first game there on October 7, 1995. They tied the Islanders 4-4. The name became TD Garden in 2005.

 It was built between 1993 and 1995. Cost of construction was $160 million U.S. That would be about $251 million U.S. today.

 Located directly next door to the old Boston Garden.

 TD Garden capacity is 17,565 for hockey, 18,624 for basketball, and 19,580 for concerts.

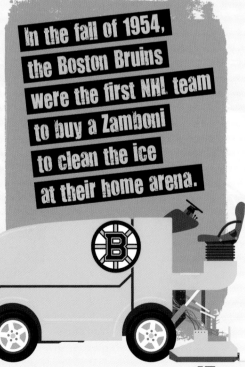

In the fall of 1954, the Boston Bruins were the first NHL team to buy a Zamboni to clean the ice at their home arena.

BOSTON'S BEST

In its history, Boston has been home to some of hockey's highest scorers, but its very best players have all been defensemen. Not only were Eddie Shore, Bobby Orr, and Raymond Bourque among the best players in the NHL at their time, they rank among the best hockey players of all time.

6'9" (206 cm)

Eddie Shore

There was no Norris Trophy for the best defenseman in the NHL when Eddie Shore starred with the Boston Bruins in the 1920s and 1930s. If there had been, Shore would have won it a lot! How good was he? Well, good enough that he was the first player in NHL history to win the Hart Trophy as league MVP four times. No other defenseman in NHL history has ever won the Hart so many times. Shore was as tough as he was talented, and though his temper sometimes got him into trouble, he was one of the NHL's first true superstars.

Standing 6'9" (206 cm), Boston's Zdeno Chara is the tallest player in NHL history. He's a big talent, too! Chara was named captain of the Bruins in 2006. He won the Norris Trophy in 2009 and led Boston to the Stanley Cup in 2011.

Bobby Orr

Many people think Bobby Orr is the greatest player in hockey history. Orr is the only defenseman to lead the NHL in scoring, and he did it twice! He scored the Stanley Cup-winning goal in overtime in 1970. He became the first player in NHL history to reach 100 assists in a single season when he had 102 in 1970–71. Orr won the Norris Trophy a record eight times in his career. He also won the Hart Trophy three times, and the Conn Smythe Trophy as playoff MVP twice. There's no telling how much more amazing Orr's career would have been if it hadn't been cut short by serious knee injuries.

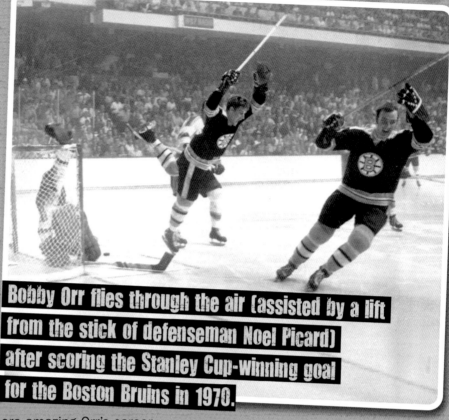

Bobby Orr flies through the air (assisted by a lift from the stick of defenseman Noel Picard) after scoring the Stanley Cup-winning goal for the Boston Bruins in 1970.

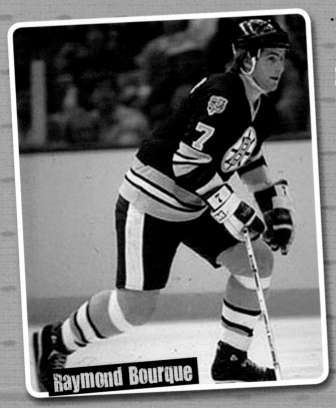

Raymond Bourque

Raymond Bourque

Raymond Bourque didn't have the offensive flair to match Bobby Orr, but he did lead the Bruins in scoring five times. Bourque played more than 20 of his 22 NHL seasons with Boston and was a star the entire time. Bourque won the Calder Trophy as rookie of the year in 1979–80 and ended his career by winning a Stanley Cup championship (with the Colorado Avalanche) in 2000–01. In between, he won the Norris Trophy five times and became the NHL's all-time leader among defensemen with 410 goals, 1,169 assists, and 1,579 points.

GREAT GOALIES

It's hard to become a great NHL team without having a great goalie. Over the years, Boston has had some of the best. These three goalies all won Stanley Cup championships with the Bruins during careers that would see them all honored with induction into the Hockey Hall of Fame.

Hall of Famer Jacques Plante had his biggest success with Montreal, St. Louis, and Toronto, but he finished his NHL career with Boston in 1973.

Tiny Thompson

Cecil Thompson is better known as "Tiny" Thompson—although at 5'10" (178 cm) the only thing really tiny about him was his goals-against average! Thompson joined the Bruins in 1928–29 and helped them win the Stanley Cup as a rookie that season. This was the lowest-scoring year in NHL history, and Thompson's goals-against average was a truly microscopic 1.15. New rules opened up the game in 1929–30, but Thompson still posted an **impressive** 2.19 average to lead the league and win the Vezina Trophy for the first of four times in his career.

Frank Brimsek

Boston fans were shocked when Tiny Thompson was traded at the start of the 1938–39 season, but the Bruins had someone ready to take over. In his first eight games after Thompson was traded, Frank Brimsek recorded seven wins and six shutouts! Boston fans loved him after that. They called Brimsek "Mr. Zero." Brimsek won the Calder Trophy as best rookie, the Vezina Trophy as best goalie, and led the Bruins to the Stanley Cup. He was never quite that good again, but Brimsek did help Boston win another Stanley Cup in 1941 and he earned the Vezina Trophy for a second time in 1942.

Gerry Cheevers' goaltending style included using his body to stop a lot of shots. After his playing career, he served as Bruins coach for five years (1980–85).

Mr. Zero

Gerry Cheevers

When Gerry Cheevers came to Boston in 1965, the Bruins were a terrible team. Soon, with stars such as Bobby Orr and Phil Esposito, Cheevers helped take Boston to the top. He always played his best when it mattered most, and helped the Bruins win the Stanley Cup in 1970 and 1972. During the 1971–72 season, Cheevers set a record that still stands by playing 32 games in a row without a loss! Cheevers was also well known for painting stitches on his mask to represent all the times it saved him from getting injured.

TROPHY WINNERS

Hockey is a team game, and the Stanley Cup is the ultimate team prize. Still, there are plenty of impressive individual awards for NHL players to win. Here's the scoop on some Boston players who've won major individual awards.

MVP

Milt Schmidt

In addition to the four Hart Trophy wins by Eddie Shore and three by Bobby Orr, these Bruins have also been named the NHL's most valuable player.

Bill Cowley (1941, 1943)
Milt Schmidt (1951)
Phil Esposito (1969, 1974)

2

When Bobby Orr won the Conn Smythe Trophy again after Boston's Stanley Cup win in 1972, he became the first player to be named playoff MVP twice.

Phil Esposito

6

Seasons in a row that Phil Esposito led the NHL in goals scored from 1969 to 1975.
There was no Maurice Richard Trophy in those days, but Esposito did win the Art Ross Trophy for leading the league in points five times in those six years.

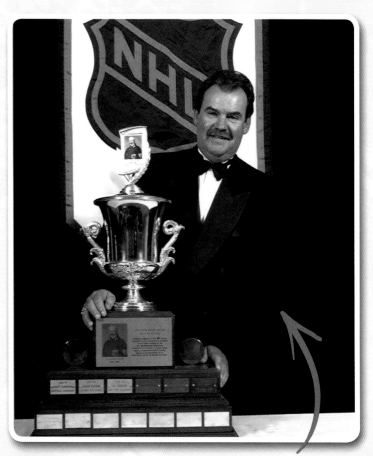

Bobby Orr and **Derek Sanderson** won the **Calder Trophy** as the NHL's rookie of the year in back-to-back seasons. Orr won it for the 1966-67 season and Sanderson won it for 1967-68.

In addition to the four **Vezina Trophy** wins by Tiny Thompson and two by Frank Brimsek, these Bruins have also been named the **NHL's best goalie:**
Pete Peeters (1983),
Tim Thomas (2009, 2011), and
Tuukka Rask (2014)

Patrice Bergeron won the **Selke Trophy** for the third time in 2014-15, becoming the fifth player to win the award for best defensive forward three times or more. He's been a finalist for the award every season from 2011-12 to 2016-17.

When Pat Burns won the Jack Adams Award as coach of the year with Boston in 1998, he became the first person to win the honor three times. Burns won it previously with Montreal in 1989 and with Toronto in 1993.

4

Major awards won by Bobby Orr for the 1969-70 season.

Orr won the Hart Trophy as MVP, the Art Ross Trophy as scoring leader, the Norris Trophy as best defenseman, and the Conn Smythe Trophy as playoff MVP. No one had ever won four trophies in one season before.

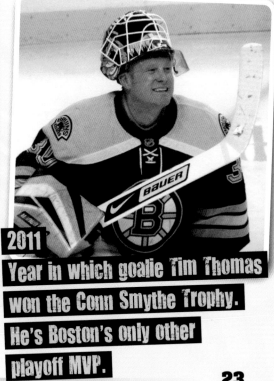

2011
Year in which goalie Tim Thomas won the Conn Smythe Trophy. He's Boston's only other playoff MVP.

BEHIND THE BENCH

It's often said that a coach is only hired to be fired. If firing the coach doesn't turn the team around, the next person to go is often the general manager. Still, a successful coach or GM can stick around for a very long time.

Art Ross

Art Ross had not just been a great hockey player when he was young. He also starred at baseball, basketball, and boxing. Later on, he was a champion motorcycle racer, a top golfer, and was excellent at shooting targets with a rifle. His best sport was football. He coached youth football teams to a few championships, but didn't do as well coaching men's teams. He also struggled in his first NHL coaching jobs with the Montreal Wanderers in 1917–18 and the Hamilton Tigers in 1922–23. Things went better for him in Boston. Ross was behind the Bruins' bench from 1924 to 1934, then again from 1936 to 1939, and from 1941 to 1945. In all, he posted a record of 387 wins, 290 losses, and 95 ties as Boston's coach. Ross's team record for coaching wins lasted until the 2015–16 season. He was also the team's general manager from 1924 until 1954.

Cam Neely became the eighth team president in Bruins history when he was named to the position on June 16, 2010. He's the only one who also played for the team too. Neely was a star scorer with the Bruins for ten seasons from 1986 to 1996.

Harvey Jackson, Art Ross and Art Jackson in Boston Garden locker room

Harry Sinden

Harry Sinden's career in the Bruins' front office has lasted even longer than Art Ross's did. Sinden first joined the Bruins as a minor league player and coach in the early 1960s. He was Boston's coach from 1966 to 1970, then returned to the team as general manager in 1972. He held that job for 28 years until 2000 and was the first GM in NHL history to have his teams win 1,000 games. Sinden was also the Bruins president from 1988 to 2006, and still serves the team as a senior adviser to the owner.

Don Cherry

You may know Don Cherry for his loud opinions—and his loud suits—as host of Coach's Corner on *Hockey Night in Canada*. Cherry was a pretty good minor league defensemen, but he only ever played one game in the NHL. He had better luck as a coach. Cherry was behind the bench in Boston from 1974 to 1979 and won the Jack Adams Award as coach of the year for the 1975–76 season.

BRUINS BITS AND PIECES

1970-71 Season
Boston set NHL records

57 Wins

121 Points

399 Goals

These are no longer NHL records, but they're still Bruins team records.

02:20

Home	Visitors
0	11

11-0
The biggest win by shutout in Bruins history when they beat Toronto on January 18, 1964.

Mel "Sudden Death" Hill

Boston's **Mel Hill** earned the nickname "**Sudden Death**" by scoring three overtime winning goals in one playoff series against the New York Rangers in 1939. Hill is the only player in NHL history to score three OT goals in one series.

The Kraut Line

Bruins forwards Milt Schmidt, Bobby Bauer, and Woody Dumart were known as "The Kraut Line." All three had grown up and played hockey together in Kitchener, Ontario, which is a city known for its German heritage. "Kraut" was a nickname for Germans, although it's considered to be offensive today.

14 Goals

scored by the Bruins on January 21, 1945, to set a team record in a 14-3 win over the New York Rangers.

83 Shots on Goal

for the Bruins to set an NHL record in a 3-2 win over Chicago on March 4, 1941. The Bruins also set a record for one period that night with 33 shots in the second.

20 Seconds

is the NHL record time for the fastest three goals by one team. John Bucyk, Ed Westfall, and Ted Green all scored between 4:50 and 5:10 of the third period in an 8-3 win against Vancouver on February 25, 1971.

15 Straight

road wins by the Bruins in 1940–41, set a team record.

WILD RIVALS

Geography and history. They're more than just subjects in school. They're what make sports rivalries so intense! In a city as old as Boston, history is important. Toronto and Montreal have both been in the NHL longer, but no two teams have played each other more times than Montreal and Boston.

Bruins vs Canadiens

As good as the Boston Bruins have usually been, the Montreal Canadiens were almost always better. Montreal and Boston have won more games and scored more goals than any teams in NHL history. Both have more than 3,000 wins in the regular season and both have scored more than 20,000 goals. They've also met in the playoffs 34 times in 100 seasons, which is far more often than any other two NHL teams. Boston has only won nine of those series—which may be one reason why Bruins fans really don't like the Canadiens! The two teams have met for the Stanley Cup seven times, and Boston has never beaten Montreal. Between 1946 and 1987, the Bruins and Canadiens met in the playoffs 18 times and the Canadiens won every single series.

The rivalry actually got off to a good start for Boston when they beat Montreal in the semifinals in 1929, and went on to win the Stanley Cup for the first time. Then, after the Bruins record-setting season of 1929–30, they met the Canadiens for the Stanley Cup and got swept. The Stanley Cup Final was only a best-of-three series that year and it marked the only time all season that Boston lost two games in a row.

Game officials separate Bruins goalie Gilles Gilbert and Habs player Steve Shutt in game 7 of the NHL Stanley Cup semifinals in 1979.

More Misery

Like those Bruins of long ago, Boston followed up its Stanley Cup win of 1970 with another record-breaking season in 1970–71. Everyone expected another championship, but when Boston faced Montreal in the very first round, the Canadiens knocked them out in seven games for another huge upset. Even so, the worst loss may have come in 1979. After losing to Montreal in the Stanley Cup Finals in 1977 and 1978, the Bruins had a chance to eliminate the Canadiens in Game 7 of the 1979 semifinals. Boston had a 3-1 lead starting the third period and led 4-3 with just 2:34 left to play. Then the Bruins got a penalty for too many men on the ice and Guy Lafleur tied the game with a power-play goal with 1:14 remaining. Montreal won the game in overtime and went on to win the Stanley Cup again. The Bruins-Canadiens rivalry led to two fan riots as well, but both of those were in Montreal in 1955 and 2008.

Glossary

brain child A creative idea coming from one person

expansion When the NHL grew, or expanded in number of teams

franchise A professional sports team

Great Depression A period of economic crisis and unemployment from 1929 to 1939

Holy Grail Something that is highly prized and desired

impressive Something that is respected or admired

rights Ownership of a contract

synthetic Made from chemical substances instead of natural materials

Further Reading

If you're a fan of the Boston Bruins, you may enjoy these books:

The Big Book of Hockey for Kids by Eric Zweig. Scholastic Canada, 2017.

The Boy in Number Four by Kara Kootstra. Puffin Canada, 2014.

Duck with the Puck by Greg Oliver and Quinn Oliver. CreateSpace Independent Publishing, 2014.

Number Four, Bobby Orr by Mike Leonetti. Raincoast Books, 2005.

The Ultimate Book of Hockey Trivia for Kids by Eric Zweig. Scholastic Canada, 2015.

Websites to Check Out

The National Hockey League's official website: **www.nhl.com**

The Boston Bruins website: **www.nhl.com/bruins**

The Hockey Hall of Fame: **www.hhof.com**

Hockey Canada's site for kids: **www.hockeycanada.ca/multimedia/kids/**